THE TRAVELLER'S QUOTATION BOOK

Confound it!
How the fellow snores.

The Traveller's Quotation Book

A Literary Tour

Edited by
JENNIFER TAYLOR

ROBERT HALE · LONDON

Preface and selection © Jennifer Taylor 1993
First published in Great Britain 1993

ISBN 0 7090 5001 1

Robert Hale Limited
Clerkenwell House
Clerkenwell Green
London EC1R 0HT

Photoset in Goudy by
Derek Doyle & Associates, Mold, Clwyd.
Printed in Hong Kong
by Bookbuilders Ltd.

Preface

ravellers can be divided into those who enjoy travelling for its own sake, and those who are happy enough when they get to their destination, but do not enjoy the journey. Every form of transport it seems has its attendant miseries. Today's traveller is likely to suffer from crowded airports, delays, congested motorways, and possibly indifferent food and accommodation. But these tribulations seem trivial compared to those of our ancestors, whose patience and endurance had to be so much greater. Reading through old travel accounts seems like a chronicle of dirty inns, rotten food – or no food at all – surly, slovenly and dishonest landlords. Plastic airline food, motorway service stations, and box-like hotel rooms (with no sea view) seem preferable on the whole.

Travelling seems to engender fears, and as the imagination goes into overdrive the terrible things that *might* happen – accidents, robbery, bandits – seem almost as real as actual dangers. As a child I was much impressed by my father's true story of how *his* grandfather, staying in a remote inn one night, had been undressing (to be precise, was just about to remove his money belt) when he looked up at a portrait above the bed and saw the eyes move. Whether he was able to secure the door, whether he slept at all, where the inn was, I don't – sadly – remember the details; but he did get away safely.

The second half of the book takes the form of a sort of Cook's tour of some of the world's well-trodden places, as each generation discovers them anew.

Travellers have often been moved to hyperbole and a gush of adjectives; equally, others have been disappointed: Dickens thought that the tower of Pisa looked much smaller than the illustration in his schoolbook showing the wonders of the world had led him to expect. Nowadays, with expectations raised by stunning travel photographs in books and magazines, how many people must be disappointed by the reality, unable to take *their* masterpiece with only a standard lens, the sun in the wrong position, scaffolding on the building, and parked cars and crowds of people in the way.

The modern proliferation of tourism is such that landscapes and local traditions are often at risk, and all good tourists should of course behave responsibly. Better still, stay at home, suggests one recent 'green' guide: is your holiday *abroad* really necessary, and if not why not spend the time relaxing at home and perhaps visiting your locality?

So settle for some hassle free, safe – and green – armchair travelling and join the travellers, truculent and adaptable, ecstatic and critical, in these pages.

JENNIFER TAYLOR

The world is a book and those who do not travel read only one page.
>ST AUGUSTINE
>*Confessions*

I think that travel comes from some deep urge to see the world, like the urge that brings up a worm in an Irish bog to see the moon when it is full.
>LORD DUNSANY
>*Holiday*, March 1951

For my part, I travel not to go anywhere, but to go. I travel for travel's sake. The great affair is to move.
>ROBERT LOUIS STEVENSON
>*Travels with a Donkey*

What people travel for is a mystery.
>T.B. MACAULAY
>in a letter to Lady Trevelyan, 21 August 1843

I am fevered with the sunset,
I am fretful with the bay,
For the wander-thirst is on me
And my soul is in Cathay.
    RICHARD HOVEY
    'The Sea Gypsy', 1896

... to give men a taste for going into foreign parts, and not loitering by their own firesides, nothing more need be done than to marry them.
    MARGARET OF NAVARRE
    The Heptameron, 1558

The little Road says, Go;
The little House says, Stay;
And oh, it's bonny here at home,
But I must go away.
    JOSEPHINE PRESTON PEABODY
    'The House and the Road'

To travel hopefully is a better thing than to arrive.
    ROBERT LOUIS STEVENSON
    Virginibus Puerisque

Travelling may be one of two things – an experience we shall always remember, or an experience which, alas, we shall never forget.
    RABBI JULIUS GORDON
    Your Sense of Humor

Travel is a foretaste of hell.
    TURKESTAN PROVERB

Travel is fatal to prejudice, bigotry, and narrow-mindedness ... Broad, wholesome, charitable views of men and things cannot be acquired by vegetating in one little corner of the earth all one's lifetime.

    MARK TWAIN
    The Innocents Abroad

I have recently been all round the world and have formed a poor opinion of it.

    SIR THOMAS BEECHAM
    in a speech at the Savoy Hotel, August 1946

He that travels far knows much.
    ENGLISH PROVERB

And men go abroad to admire the heights of mountains, the mighty billows of the sea, the long courses of rivers, the vast compass of the ocean, and the circular motion of the stars, and yet pass themselves by.

> ST AUGUSTINE
> *Confessions*

What canst thou see elsewhere which thou seest not here? Behold the heavens and the earth, and all the elements; for of these are all things made.

> THOMAS À KEMPIS
> *De Imitatione Christi*

See one promontory, one mountain, one sea, one river, and see all.

> SOCRATES

'*Ecco!*' she says. 'Tell me this – tell me the truth – why do you come here at all? Why do you travel?' To this I reply, of course, that we travel to see the country. 'To see the country!' she repeats, clasping her withered hands. '*Gran' Dio!* Have you, then, no mountains and no trees in England?'

> AMELIA EDWARDS, questioned in the Dolomites
> *Untrodden Peaks and Unfrequented Valleys*, 1873

What benefit has travel of itself ever been able to give anyone? ... It merely holds our attention for a moment by a certain novelty.

> SENECA
> *Epistulae ad Lucilium*

'Travel' is the name of a modern disease ... The patient grows restless in the early spring and starts rushing from one travel agent to another, collecting useless information.
GEORGE MIKES
How to Be Inimitable

Travel, so broadening at first, contracts the mind.
PAUL THEROUX

Those who travel heedlessly from place to place, observing only their distance from each other, and attending only to their accommodation at the inn at night, set out fools, and will certainly return so.

> LORD CHESTERFIELD
> *Letters to His Son*, 30 October 1747

He travelled here, he travelled there;
But not the value of a hair
Was head or heart the better.

> WILLIAM WORDSWORTH
> 'Peter Bell'

Travel makes a wise man better, but a fool worse.

> THOMAS FULLER
> *Gnomologia*

It is a pity that people travel in foreign countries; it narrows their minds so much.

> G.K. CHESTERTON

It appears that many people when they travel really see nothing at all except the reflection of their own ideas.

> STEPHEN LEACOCK
> Canadian humorist

Travel, in the younger sort, is a part of education; in the elder, a part of experience. He that travelleth into a country, before he hath some entrance into the language, goeth to school, and not to travel.

> FRANCIS BACON
> *Essays:* 'Of Travel'

If a young man is wild, and must run after women and bad company, it is better this should be done abroad, as, on his return, he can break off such connections, and begin at home a new man.

> SAMUEL JOHNSON
> Boswell's *Life of Johnson*

Young men should travel, if but to amuse
Themselves.

> BYRON
> *Don Juan*

Led by my hand, he saunter'd Europe around,
And gather'd ev'ry vice on Christian ground.

> ALEXANDER POPE
> *The Dunciad*

... the greatest blockheads in nature ... their whole business abroad (as far as I can perceive) being to buy new cloaths, in which they shine in some obscure coffee-house, where they are sure of meeting only one another; and after the important conquest of some waiting gentlewoman of an opera Queen ... return to England excellent judges of men and manners ... and no more instructed than they might have been at home by the help of a map.

> LADY MARY WORTLEY MONTAGU, of young
> Englishmen on the Grand Tour, in a letter

How much a dunce that has been sent to roam
Excels a dunce that has been kept at home.

> WILLIAM COWPER
> *The Progress of Error*

The perpetual lamentations after beef and beer, the stupid, bigoted contempt for everything foreign, an insurmountable incapacity for acquiring even a few words of any language, rendered him, like all other English servants, an incumbrance. I do assure you, the plague of speaking for him, the comforts he required (more than myself by far), the pilaws (a Turkish dish of rice and meat) which he could not eat, the wines which he could not drink, the beds where he could not sleep, and the long list of calamities, such as stumbling horses, want of *tea*!!! &c., which assailed him, would have made a lasting source of laughter to a spectator, and inconvenience to a master.

BYRON, complaining about his servant William
Fletcher in a letter to his mother, 14 January 1811

Those who have seen an English family-carriage on the continent must have remarked the sensation it produces. It is an epitome of England; a little morsel of the old Island rolling about the world ... the ruddy faces gaping from the windows ... and then the dickeys loaded with well-dressed servants beef-fed and bluff; looking down from their heights with contempt on all the world around; profoundly ignorant of the country and the people, and devoutly certain that everything not English must be wrong.

WASHINGTON IRVING
Tales of a Traveller

Yes, we all flock the one after the other, we faithful English folks. We can buy Harvey Sauce, and Cayenne Pepper, and Morison's Pills in every city in the world. We carry our nation everywhere with us; and are in our island, wherever we go.

W.M. THACKERAY
The Kickleburys on the Rhine

To go to France and Italy and there converse with none but English people, and merely that you have it to say that you have been in these countries is certainly absurd.
JOHN MOORE
A View of Society and Manners in Italy, 1792

If you reject the food, ignore the customs, fear the religion and avoid the people, you might better stay home.
JAMES A. MICHENER
Holiday, March 1956

Nothing so necessary for travellers as languages.
ENGLISH PROVERB

Travel teaches toleration.
> BENJAMIN DISRAELI
> *Contarini Fleming*

For my part I try to take things as they come, with cheerfulness, and when I cannot get a dinner to suit my taste I endeavour to get a taste to suit my dinner.
> WASHINGTON IRVING
> *Journal of a Tour Through France and Italy*, 1804-5

I flatter myself I have already improved considerably by my travels. First, I can swallow gruel soup, egg soup, and all manner of soups, without making faces much. Secondly, I can pretty well live without tea.
> ANNA LETITIA BARBAULD
> English poet and bluestocking
> in a letter to Miss Belshan, 21 October 1785, from
> Geneva

A traveller must have the back of an ass to bear all, a tongue like the tail of a dog to flatter all, the mouth of a hog to eat what is set before him.
> THOMAS NASHE
> *Works*

How often persons who have traveled around the world tell you so earnestly that they found a place in Venice where they served American ham and eggs.
> ALFRED CARL HOTTES
> *Garden Fads and Fancies*

I dislike feeling at home when I am abroad.
> BERNARD SHAW

The whole object of travel is not to set foot on foreign land; it is at last to set foot on one's own country as a foreign land.

    G.K. CHESTERTON

The more I see of other countries, the more I love my own.

    Mme DE STAËL
    Corinne

A wise traveller never despises his own country.

    GOLDONI
    Pamela

I should like to spend the whole of my life in travelling abroad, if I could anywhere borrow another life to spend afterwards at home.

    WILLIAM HAZLITT
    Table-Talk: 'On Going a Journey'

The urge to go places has always been with me, but although I have journeyed the world and home again, the small horizons of my own country are those that call most insistently and satisfy me best.

    LESLIE THOMAS
    The Hidden Places of Britain

I solemnly cursed every moment I had spent wandering foolishly about the world, and I swore that if ever I saw Dover Cliffs again I would never leave them.

    H.V. MORTON, feeling homesick in Palestine in 1923
    In Search of England

Journey over all the universe in a map, without the expense and fatigue of travelling, without suffering the inconveniences of heat, cold, hunger, and thirst.

MIGUEL DE CERVANTES
Don Quixote

The world is a country which no one yet ever knew by description; one must travel through it oneself to be acquainted with it.

LORD CHESTERFIELD
Letters to His Son, 2 October 1747

I doubt whether I ever read any description of scenery which gave me an idea of the place described.

ANTHONY TROLLOPE
Australia and New Zealand

But damn description, it is always disgusting.

BYRON
in a letter to Francis Hodgson, 6 August 1809

Books of travels will be good in proportion to what a man has previously in his mind; his knowing what to observe; his power of contrasting one mode of life with another.

> SAMUEL JOHNSON
> Boswell's *Life of Johnson*

A traveller may lie with authority.

> ENGLISH PROVERB

They told of prodigies, as one who has returned from far countries, the force of whirlwinds, and unheard-of-birds, monsters of the deep, uncertain combinations of men and beasts – things seen, or believed through fear.

> TACITUS
> *Annals*

Like all great travellers, I have seen more than I remember, and remember more than I have seen.

> BENJAMIN DISRAELI

A class of men who are exceedingly tiresome are those who, having travelled, talk of nothing but their adventures, the countries which they have seen or traversed, the dangers, whether real or fictitious, which they have encountered.

> ST JOHN BAPTIST DE LA SALLE
> *The Rules of Christian Manners and Civility*, 1695

Travel is the most private of pleasures. There is no greater bore than the travel bore. We do not in the least want to hear what he has seen in Hong Kong.

> VICTORIA SACKVILLE-WEST
> *Passenger to Tehran*

The world is his who has money to go over it.
RALPH WALDO EMERSON
Conduct of Life: Wealth

I think that to get under the surface and really appreciate
the beauty of any country, one has to go there poor.
GRACE MOORE
You're Only Human Once, 1944

See that you never want two bags very full, that is one of
patience and another of money.
JOHN FLORIO
Second Frutes, 1591

The heaviest baggage for a traveller is an empty purse.
GERMAN PROVERB

Americans have always been eager for travel, that being
how they got to the New World in the first place.
OTTO FRIEDRICH
Time, 22 April 1985

One of the main troubles about going to Europe is that no
one wants to hear about your trip when you get back home.
ART BUCHWALD
Vogue, 1 April 1954

Americans are people who prefer the Continent to their
own country but refuse to learn its languages.
E.V. LUCAS
Wanderings and Diversions

'What hotel do you go to?' I asked of Lady Kicklebury.

'We go to the Saint-Antoine, of course. Everybody goes to the Saint-Antoine,' her ladyship said. 'We propose to rest here; to do the Rubenses; and to proceed to Cologne to-morrow.'

W.M. THACKERAY
The Kickleburys on the Rhine

As for churches, and pictures, I have stared at them till my brains are like a guide-book.

BYRON in Brussels
in a letter to Augusta Leigh, 1 May 1816

I realize that the only thing that has hitherto kept us going has been that remaining sense of obligation to identify – Baedeker in hand – new regions, museums, palaces and ruins; since this obligation does not exist here I am simply drowning in a life of ease.

SIGMUND FREUD
Letters

Somnolent through landscapes and by trees …
they alter as they enter foreign cities –
the terrible tourists with their empty eyes
longing to be filled with monuments.

P.K. PAGE, Canadian poet
'The Permanent Tourists', *The Metal and the Flower*

The traveler was active; he went strenuously in search of people, of adventure, of experience. The tourist is passive; he expects interesting things to happen to him. He goes 'sightseeing'.

DANIEL J. BOORSTIN
The Image, 1962

There are tourists incapable of looking at a masterpiece for its own sake. They bow into a camera, snap experiences never had, then rush home and develop these celluloid events so as to see where they've been.

> NED ROREM
> 'Listening and Hearing', *Music from Inside and Out*,
> 1967

There is nothing wrong with being a tourist, nothing uncomfortable about it if you are insensitive to how funny you look to the natives and simply enjoy how funny they look to you.

> JANE RULE, Canadian novelist
> 'Funny People', *A Hot-Eyed Moderate*

A wise traveller desires to act like those animals that take on the colour, the form, the exact appearance of the objects that surround them.

> MAURICE BARRÈS
> *Voyage de Sparte*

In a café in Rhodes three Englishwomen walked in wearing the most outlandish holiday clothes and Panama hats, with lots of raincoats and cameras and walking sticks and rucksacks. They stood about looking for a waiter and one said in a loud voice, 'How do we attract attention?'

> ELIZABETH TAYLOR, novelist
> in a letter to Robert Liddell in 1956

The tourist may complain of other tourists; but he would be lost without them.

> AGNES REPPLIER
> *Times and Tendencies*

The soul of a journey is liberty, perfect liberty, to think, feel, do just as one pleases. We go a journey chiefly to be free of all impediments and of all inconveniences; to leave ourselves behind, much more to get rid of others.

WILLIAM HAZLITT
Table-Talk, 'On Going a Journey'

Travelling in the company of those we love is home in motion.

LEIGH HUNT
The Indicator

He travels the fastest who travels alone.

RUDYARD KIPLING
The Winners

I have found out that there aint no surer way to find out whether you like people or hate them than to travel with them.

MARK TWAIN
Tom Sawyer Abroad

Travelling with anyone is a very ticklish business ... What is your thrill may be my bore ... I cannot imagine what fire and pillage I would commit if anyone were in a position to keep me looking at things longer than I wanted to look.

CORNELIA STRATTON PARKER
English Summer

I believe to travel is the most likely way to make a solitude agreeable, and not tiresome.

LADY MARY WORTLEY MONTAGU
in a letter to Wortley Montagu, August 1712

The Natural tenderness and Delicacy of our Constitution, added to the many Dangers we are subject to from your Sex, renders it almost impossible for a Single Lady to travel without injury to her character.

ABIGAIL ADAMS
in a letter to Isaac Smith jun., 20 April 1771

'A guide?' she exclaims ... 'Not I! What do I want with a guide? I have carried my own knapsack and found my own way through France, through England, through Italy, through Palestine ... Fatigue is nothing to me – distance is nothing to me – danger is nothing to me. I have been taken by brigands before now. What of that? ... I made friends of my brigands – I painted all their portraits – I spent a month with them; and we parted, the best comrades in the world.'

AMELIA EDWARDS, encountering an indomitable
German lady in the Dolomites
Untrodden Peaks and Unfrequented Valleys, 1873

I am much pleased that you are going on a very long journey, which may by proper conduct restore your health and prolong your life. Observe these rules: 1. Turn all care out of your head as soon as you mount the chaise. 2. Do not think about frugality; your health is worth more than it can cost. 3. Do not continue any day's journey to fatigue.

SAMUEL JOHNSON
in a letter to Henry Perkins, 28 July 1782

If you look like your passport photo, then in all probability you need the journey.

EARL WILSON

'The truth is,' pursued Mr Culpepper, 'I am travelling for my health, and therefore I am taking cross-roads, and stopping at out of the way places. For there is no health to be got by staying in cities, and putting up at crowded hotels.'

ELIZA LESLIE
Pencil Sketches, or *Outlines of Character and Manners*, 1837

'Always before beginning to pack', my Uncle would say, 'make a list ... Take a piece of paper ... put down on it everything you can possibly require ... Imagine yourself in bed; what have you got on? Very well, put it down – together with a change. You get up; what do you do? Wash yourself. What do you wash yourself with? Soap; put down soap. Go on till you have finished.'

> JEROME K. JEROME
> sound advice from Uncle Podger, *Three Men on the Bummell*

Very refreshing

There is no denying the fact ... that dirt and grease are great protectors of the skin against inclement weather, and that therefore the leader of a party should not be too exacting about the appearance of his less warmly-clad followers.

> FRANCIS GALTON
> *The Art of Travel*, 1854

Is there *anything* as horrible as *starting* on a trip? Once you're off, that's all right, but the last moments are earthquake and convulsion, and the feeling that you are a snail being pulled off your rock.

> ANNE MORROW LINDBERGH
> *Hour of Gold, Hour of Lead*

My passion for travel cools when I consider that it consists entirely of departures and arrivals.

> MARQUIS DE CUSTINE
> writing in 1839

'Elizabeth, take care of Miss Jane … Hicks! Hicks! for heaven's sake mind the babies! – My love, *do* take the cloaks and umbrellas, and give a hand to Fanny and Lucy; and I wish you would speak to the hackney-coachmen, dear; they want fifteen shillings, and count the packages, love – twenty-seven packages, – and bring little Flo; where's little Flo? – Flo! Flo! …'

> W.M. THACKERAY
> departure time on the quayside, *The Paris Sketch Book*

The married Briton on a tour is but a luggage overseer; his luggage is his morning thought, and his nightly terror.

> W.M. THACKERAY
> *The Kickleburys on the Rhine*

The coolie is yet to be discovered who would carry a carpetbag, and a bandbox does not precisely meet the views of a camel.

> EMILY EDEN
> in a letter from India 21 October 1837, *Up the Country*, 1866

People were tumbling over each other in their haste, and making impossible demands, each one being anxious to have his luggage produced first, though the said luggage might be at the bottom of the hold.

ISABELLA BIRD
arrival time, *The Englishwoman in America*, 1856

There is no moment of delight in any pilgrimage like the beginning of it, when the traveller is settled simply as to his destination, and commits himself to his unknown fate and all the anticipations of adventures before him.

CHARLES DUDLEY WARNER
Baddeck and That Sort of Thing

Postilion, drive slowly – Take care you do not upset us – Don't go to sleep, postilion – Do not drive so near the river / the precipice / the ditch – The postilion is drunk / impertinent / foolhardy – The carriage is near the precipice – One of the wheels is off – Oh dear! The postilion has been thrown down – I am afraid he has broken his leg / his arm – Ask for a surgeon – It rains in torrents – It lightens / it thunders – It is impossible to travel in such weather – The lightning has struck that tree – This is quite a hurricane – I am really much alarmed.

> *Murray's Handbook of Travel-Talk*, 1874
> some useful phrases for the traveller abroad

The deaf postilion

We lost our way in the dark, or rather twilight, not far from Ghent, by the stupidity of the postilion ..., which produced an alarm of intended robbery amongst the uninitiated, whom I could not convince that four or five well-armed people were not immediately to be plundered and anatomized by a single person.

> BYRON
> in a letter to Augusta Leigh from Brussels, 1 May 1816

We hired a sort of open baggage-wagon for the trip down the valley to Chamonix, and then devoted an hour to dining. This gave the driver time to get drunk ... Down came his whip, and away we clattered. I never had such a shaking up in my life. The recent flooding rains had washed the road clear away in places, but we never stopped, we never slowed down, for anything.

> MARK TWAIN
> *A Tramp Abroad*

At one time we were all flung together in a heap at the bottom of the coach, and at another we were crushing our heads against the roof. Now, one side was down deep in the mire, and we were holding on to the other. Now, the coach ... was rearing up in the air.

> CHARLES DICKENS, travelling in Ohio
> *American Notes*

The Coach carries only 4 inside Passengers. We had a very fat Woman with a Dog and many band boxes, which much incommoded us.

> REVD JAMES WOODFORDE
> *Diary*, 28 June 1793

The road not very bad, but the hills severe and our miserable horses nearly gruelled, almost fainting from thirst and fatigue, all abroad scrambling and staggering all over

the place. Once in a narrow part of the road the wheel tottered on the edge of a bank. We yawed about frightfully, the horses were too much done to pull straight or steady. Another lurch and we should have gone head over heels into the field below.

REVD FRANCIS KILVERT on the road in Cornwall
Diary, 29 July 1870

The landau rocks and rolls like a ship at sea. Every moment the road becomes worse, and the blaze of noonday heat more intolerable. Presently we come upon a gang of road-makers some two hundred in number, women and children as well as men ... They pause in their work, and stare at us as if we were creatures from another world. 'You are the first travellers who have come up this way,' says the overseer, as we pass by. 'You must be Inglese!'

AMELIA EDWARDS in the Dolomites
Untrodden Peaks and Unfrequented Valleys, 1873

Surely never did small hero experience greater misadventures than I did on the first two or three days of my travelling. Twice did my horse run away with me, and greatly endanger the breaking my neck on the first day. On the second I drove two hours through as copious a rain as ever I have seen, without meeting with a single house to which I could repair for shelter. On the third, in going through Pamunkey, being unacquainted with the ford, I passed through water so deep as to run over the cushion as I sat on it.

THOMAS JEFFERSON
in a letter to John Page, 25 May 1776

Going down the hill on the other side was no easy task. As Dr Johnson was a great weight, the two guides agreed that he should ride the horses alternately.

JAMES BOSWELL
Journal of a Tour to the Hebrides

The swiftest traveller is he that goes afoot.
>HENRY DAVID THOREAU
>*Walden: Economy*

[Walking] certainly is, especially in a mountainous and hilly country, the best and pleasantest way, as there are greater opportunities of seeing the country ... Indeed, in some of the parts we travelled through, a wheel carriage had never been seen, and the only conveyance we could have got would have been welch Ponies, and I had far rather trust to my own legs than these animals.
>JAMES PLUMPTRE
>*Journals*, describing a visit to North Wales in 1792

I would recommend early rising, and always turning over a good stage before breakfast. This I never failed to do when a young man; and even now I like walking before breakfast best when on a journey. Fifteen or twenty miles before nine o'clock was my ordinary arrangement.
>REVD THOMAS GRIERSON
>*Autumnal Rambles Among the Scottish Mountains*, 1850

The sun blazes overhead and hours pass, while you trudge through the fiery inferno; scintillations of heat rise from the stones and still you crawl onwards, breathless and footsore, till eyes are dazed and senses reel.
>NORMAN DOUGLAS walking along a dried out
>torrent-bed
>*Old Calabria*

Having walked now twenty miles in a broiling day I thought it high time to take some refreshment, and inquired the way to the inn ... There I dined in a grand saloon amidst a great deal of fashionable company, who probably conceiving from my heated and dusty appearance, that I was some poor fellow travelling on foot from motives of economy, surveyed me with looks of the most supercilious disdain.

> GEORGE BORROW
> *Wild Wales*

Landlords of most of the big public houses make it abundantly clear that a foot-borne man is as unwelcome among hard-drinking, car-driving customers as the gypsies are.

> JOHN HILLABY
> *Journey through Britain*

I was determined, if not to camp out, at least to have the means of camping out in my possession; for there is nothing more harassing to an easy mind than the necessity of reaching shelter by dusk ... A tent, above all for a solitary traveller, is troublesome to pitch ... A sleeping-sack, on the other hand, is always ready.

> ROBERT LOUIS STEVENSON
> *Travels with a Donkey in the Cévennes*

The only part of my luggage which puzzled the *douane* officer was the sleeping-bag. He smelt it suspiciously, the waterproof cloth having a strong odour. 'What is it for?' 'To sleep in.' He put his nose down again, and apparently uncertain in his own mind as to what course to pursue, called for another official, who desired me to unroll it. 'And you sleep in that big bag?' was the question. 'Yes.' 'What extraordinary people the English are!'

> FREDERICK BURNABY, travelling in Russia
> *A Ride to Khiva*, 1876

'I have it!' exclaimed Harris; 'a bicycle tour!'

George looked doubtful. 'There's a lot of uphill about a bicycle tour,' said he, 'and the wind is against you.'

'So there is downhill, and the wind behind you,' said Harris.

'I've never noticed it,' said George.

JEROME K. JEROME
Three Men on the Bummell

I am suddenly confronted by a pond of liquid mud that bars my farther progress down the mountain ... There is no way to get around it; perpendicular walls of rock and slippery yellow clay rise sheer from the water on either side. There is evidently nothing for it but to disrobe without more ado and try the depth ... After waddling about in it for fifteen minutes, first finding a fordable place, and then carrying clothes and wheel across, I emerge on to the bank formed by the land-slip looking as woe-begone a specimen of humanity as can well be imagined.

> THOMAS STEVENS
> *Around the World on a Bicycle*, 1888

Crossed the Loire in freezing weather and rode upstream on the embankment towards Sully where I bought a large wound-dressing in a *droguerie* for my bottom ...; and which, without a mirror, I stuck on with some difficulty behind a hedge.

> ERIC NEWBY
> *A Traveller's Life*

A curse on all barbed wire as a villainous tearer of knickerbockers.

> JOHN FOSTER FRASER
> *Round the World on a Wheel*, 1899

An elephant is far the most difficult animal to sit that I have ever been on. You feel at first rather as if you were in a light boat lying at anchor in seas a little choppy after a capful of wind.

> GERTRUDE BELL
> in a letter from India, 18 January 1903

I have rid upon an Elephant since I came to this court, determining one day (by Gods leave) to have my picture expressed in my next Booke, sitting upon an Elephant.

> THOMAS CORYAT
> *Coryat's Crudities*, 1611

He who travels not by sea knows not what the fear of God is.

ENGLISH PROVERB

I now saw what I never saw before, a prodigious sea, with immense billows coming upon a vessel, so as that it seemed hardly possible to escape. There was something grandly horrible in the sight. I am glad I have seen it once.

JAMES BOSWELL

crossing between Skye and Mull, *Journal of a Tour to the Hebrides*, 3 October 1773

The first great wave which came over the ship threw everybody down in every direction. Poor little Affie [Alfred] was thrown down and sent rolling over the deck, and was drenched, for the deck was swimming with water. Albert told me it was quite frightful to see the enormous waves rising like a wall above the sides of the ship.

QUEEN VICTORIA on board the *Victoria and Albert*
between Ireland and Scotland
Leaves from the Journal of Our Life in the Highlands, 12 August 1849

Two days ago I was nearly lost in a Turkish ship of war, owing to the ignorance of the captain and crew, though the storm was not violent. Fletcher yelled after his wife, the Greeks called on all the saints, the Mussulmans on Alla; the captain burst into tears and ran below deck, telling us to call on God.

BYRON

in a letter to his mother from Prevesa, 12 November 1809

Once – once – I found myself on deck. I don't know how I got there, or what possessed me to go there, but there I was; … I found myself standing, when a gleam of consciousness came upon me, holding on to something. I don't know what. I think it was the boatswain: or it may have been the pump … I can't say how long I had been there; whether a day or a minute … I could not even make out which was the sea, and which the sky, for the horizon seemed drunk, and was flying wildly about, in all directions.

CHARLES DICKENS
crossing the Atlantic in January, *American Notes*

Never, never be tempted to take a sea voyage. It is quite the nastiest thing you can take – I have had three days of it now, so I know.

ANNA BUCHAN
writing home from the *Scotia*

Most of the passengers were sea-sick, and those who were not so were promenading the wet, sooty deck in the rain, in a uniform of oilskin coats and caps.

... Dinner on a plentiful scale was served at one, but out of 300 passengers only about 30 were able to avail themselves of it.

ISABELLA BIRD
The Englishwoman in America, 1856

When does this place get to England?

BEA LILLIE, on board the *Queen Mary*
quoted in *New York Times*, 3 September 1967

Crash went the lamp, which was suspended from the ceiling, as a huge wave struck the ship, making her reel and stagger, and shrieks of terror followed this event, which left us in almost total darkness. Rush came another heavy wave, sweeping up the saloon, carrying chairs and stools before it, and as rapidly retiring ... Wave after wave now struck the ship. I heard the captain say the sea was making a clean breach over her, and order the deck-load overboard. Shortly after, the water, sweeping in from above, put out the engine fires.

> ISABELLA BIRD
> *The Englishwoman in America*, 1856

By the lurid light without, I beheld a crowd of Chinese junks. Beside myself with terror, I flew back to the captain, crying, 'Oh, they are pirates! they are pirates!' And they were indeed pirates – those terrible pirates which scour the Chinese seas, and are so famous for their cruelties ... Three junks, each manned by thirty or forty ruffians, surrounded the *Caldera*. These creatures seemed like demons, born of the tempest, and bent upon completing our destruction. Having boarded the *Caldera* by means of grappling-hooks, they were now dancing an infernal dance upon deck, and uttering cries which sounded like nothing human.

> FANNY LOVIOT
> *A Lady's Captivity Among Chinese Pirates*, a true
> account, translated by Amelia Edwards, 1854

Four hoarse blasts of a ship's whistle still raise the hair on my neck and set my feet to tapping.

> JOHN STEINBECK
> *Travels with Charley*

Ever since childhood, when I lived within earshot of the Boston and Maine, I have seldom heard a train go by and not wished I was on it. Those whistles sing bewitchment: railways are irresistible bazaars.

> PAUL THEROUX
> *The Great Railway Bazaar*

The express from Marseilles, which I took at Orange, was full to overflowing; and the only refuge I could find was an inside angle in a carriage laden with Germans, who had command of the windows, which they occupied as strongly as they have been known to occupy other strategical positions.

> HENRY JAMES
> *A Little Tour in France*

'Can you not get further away from me, sir?' – 'It is impossible, madam; my neighbour, here, is very stout' – ... 'Please have the goodness to keep your elbows down' – ... 'I really must request you to move a little, madam, I can hardly breathe' ... 'Here we are at our destination, God be thanked!'

> English conversation for the use of German travellers
> JEROME K. JEROME
> *Three Men on the Bummel*

At Lucknow I changed trains and found myself sharing an eight-seater compartment with seventeen Gurkha soldiers going home on leave. Each was carrying a vast amount of kit.

> DERVLA MURPHY
> *The Waiting Land*

A railway journey is a good deal like a sea voyage; its miseries fade from the mind as soon as you arrive.

> HENRY JAMES
> *A Little Tour in France*

I detest *all* forms of travel with an unassuageable loathing that grows greater, not less, with the passing years ... Every kind of transport, from the car to the Concorde, I find unbearable.

> BERNARD LEVIN, who *is* happy when he gets there
> *Enthusiasms*

Travelling around in a little tin box isolates one from the people and the atmosphere of the place ... I found myself eyeing with envy all rucksacks and tents.

> ROSALIND FRANKLIN
> English physicist

Methods of locomotion have improved greatly in recent years, but places to go remain about the same.
DON HEROLD

Modern air travel means less time spent in transit. That time is now spent in transit lounges.
P.J. O'ROURKE
Holidays in Hell, 1988

Airline insurance replaces the fear of death with the comforting prospect of cash.
CECIL BEATON
on the automatic insurance machines in US airline terminals
It Gives Me Great Pleasure

… the limitless jet-lag purgatory of Immigration and Baggage at Heathrow.
MONICA DICKENS
'A Modern Dickens Writes about Returning to the Land of Her Great-Grandfather', *Christian Science Monitor*, 13 March 1986

A plane is a bad place for an all-out sleep, but a good place to begin rest and recovery from the trip to the faraway places you've been, a decompression chamber between Here and There.
SHANA ALEXANDER

All travelling becomes dull in exact proportion to its rapidity.
JOHN RUSKIN

In landing we had to suffer the usual impositions incident to such situations – boatmen, porters, waiters, &c all put in their claims and tried to pluck as many feathers from us as possible … I find it is generally in vain to remonstrate in such circumstances … The traveller when in haste to proceed – or when overcome with lassitude & fatigue – prefers rather to suffer in his purse then to engage in altercations.

> WASHINGTON IRVING, on landing at Gravesend
> *Journal of a Tour Through France and Italy*, 8 October 1804

Reader, please to bear in mind that as all bills must be paid, it is much more comfortable to pay them with a smile than with a frown, and that it is much better by giving sixpence, or a shilling to a poor servant, which you will never miss at the year's end, to be followed from the door of an inn by good wishes, than by giving nothing to be pursued by cutting silence, or yet more cutting H'm!

> GEORGE BORROW
> *Wild Wales*

Speaking of presents and articles for payment, as of money, it is essential to have a great quantity and variety of *small change*, wherewith the traveller can pay for small services, for carrying messages, for draughts of milk, pieces of meat, &c. Beads, shells, tobacco, needles, awls, cotton caps, handkerchiefs, clasp-knives, small axes, spear and arrow heads, generally answer this purpose.

> FRANCIS GALTON
> *The Art of Travel*, 1854

We came on to the inn at Glenelg. There was no provender for our horses; so they were sent to grass, with a man to watch them. A maid showed us up stairs into a room damp and dirty, with bare walls, a variety of bad smells, a coarse black greasy fir table, and forms of the same kind; and out of a wretched bed started a fellow from his sleep, like Edgar in King Lear, 'Poor Tom's a cold'. This inn was furnished with not a single article that we could either eat or drink.

> JAMES BOSWELL
> *Journal of a Tour to the Hebrides*, 31 August 1773

Unfortunately there was hardly anything to eat, and there was only tea, and two miserable starved Highland chickens, without any potatoes! No pudding, and no *fun*.

> QUEEN VICTORIA at the inn at Dalwhinnie
> *Leaves from the Journal of Our Life in the Highlands*, 8 October 1861

The house was dismal and dirty beyond all description; the bed-cloaths filthy enough to turn the stomach of a muleteer; and the victuals cooked in such a manner, that even a Hottentot could not have beheld them without loathing. We had sheets of our own, which were spread upon a mattrass, and here I took my repose wrapped in a greatcoat, if that could be called repose which was interrupted by the innumerable stings of vermin.

> TOBIAS SMOLLETT at a small village near Arezzo
> *Travels through France and Italy*

Fastidiousness is a wretched travelling companion.

> WILLIAM WORDSWORTH
> *Guide to the Lakes*, 1810

The sleeping-room was furnished with two beds. I had one; and I will own I was a little abashed to find a young man and his wife and child in the act of mounting into the other ... I kept my eyes to myself.

> ROBERT LOUIS STEVENSON
> *Travels with a Donkey in the Cévennes*

I forthwith took possession of my bed-chamber – got a good fire – order'd supper; and was thanking Heaven it was no worse when a voiture arrived with a lady in it and her servant-maid.

As there was no other bed-chamber in the house, the hostess, without much nicety, led them into mine, telling them, as she usher'd them in, that there was nobody in it but an English gentleman – that there were two good beds in it, and a closet within the room which held another.

> LAURENCE STERNE
> a delicate case for a gentleman, *A Sentimental Journey through France and Italy*

The hard, dirty floor we hailed with delight, and slept heavily for five hours. At some of the post-stations other travellers may be found, of various ages and of both sexes, and they all have to find places on the one floor for the night ... As to the state of the atmosphere in the morning, after a number of people, enveloped in dirty sheepskins, have been enjoying repose, and the room without a chink of ventilation, I leave to the reader's imagination.

> KATE MARSDEN
> *On Sledge and Horseback to Outcast Siberian Lepers*, 1892

A traveller should always be furnished with some iron machine to shut his door on the inside ...; for it frequently happens that the doors of the lodging-rooms have neither locks nor bolts, and opportunity, according to the old proverb, makes the thief.

> SIR THOMAS NUGENT
> *The Grand Tour*, 1749

I confess I did not feel well at ease in this lodging. The wild and solitary situation of the house, the rough looks & manners of the people and their apparent indigence were sufficient to awaken disagreeable sensations, particularly as I knew this road had been much infested by robberies within the short space of eighteen months or two years.

> WASHINGTON IRVING on the road near Marseilles
> *Journal of a Tour Through France and Italy*, 11
> September 1804

Soon after midnight I woke, not with a start, but with the consciousness of which I had often read ..., that I was not alone in the tent. The darkness was black as pitch and thick as velvet; and though I listened intently without moving a muscle, I heard no sound. Half unconsciously I put out my left hand and dropped it between the bed and the canvas wall of the tent which the bed all but touched. It fell plumb ... on the shaven head of a man. I could feel the prickle of the sprouting hair against my palm. But in the same moment the object slid out of my grasp and a rustle indicated the stealthy withdrawal of the intruder ... Springing up, I struck a match, seized my revolver, and dashed in my pyjamas out of the tent.

> LORD CURZON
> *Tales of Travel*, 1923

A few days later we set out on our return to Florence, and as we happened to lie at a place on this side of Chioggia, ... the landlord demanded his reckoning before we went to bed; upon telling him, that in other places it was customary to pay in the morning, he answered, I insist upon being paid over night, and as I think proper ... Tribolo trembled with fear, and signified to me to be quiet, lest the man should do something worse; so we paid him in the manner he required, and went to bed. We had very fine new beds, with every thing else new, and in the utmost elegance; notwithstanding all this I never closed my eyes the whole night, my mind being entirely engaged by the thought how I should revenge the insolent treatment of our landlord: now it came into my head to set the house on fire, and now to kill four good horses which the fellow had in his stable. I thought it was no difficult matter to put either design in execution, but did not see how I could easily secure my own and my fellow-traveller's escape afterwards: at last I resolved to put our baggage onto the ferry, and desiring my companions to go on board, ... I went back to the inn and ... went up stairs, carrying with me a little knife, which had an exceeding sharp edge, and with it I cut the four beds, till I had done damage to the value of upwards of fifty crowns.

> BENVENUTO CELLINI
> *Life*, translated by Sir Thomas Nugent, 1771

The plumbing in these Italian hotels is barbaric ... The water running away out of the basins makes a perfect hades of a row – so much so that the basins couldn't be used at night without waking the person in the next room.

> ARNOLD BENNETT
> *Journals*, 15 February 1926, from Pisa

Is forbidden to steal towels, please. If you are not person to do such is please not to read notice.

>   sign in a Tokyo hotel
>   quoted in *Holiday*, 5 May 1969

As compared with Continental hotels, English hotels may be said as a rule to excel in beds, cleanliness, and sanitary arrangements, while their cuisine is on the whole inferior. The English table d'hôte dinner is usually dear and seldom so good as its prototype on the Continent.

>   KARL BAEDEKER
>   *Great Britain Handbook for Travellers*, 1887

'Schlafen Sie Wohl' – 'Sleep well'.

This ain't the Waldorf; if it was you wouldn't be here.

>   humorous notice found in American country hotels
>   *c*. 1900

I suggested that she take a trip round the world. 'Oh, I know,' returned the lady, yawning with ennui, 'but there's so many other places I want to see first.'

S.J. PERELMAN
Westward Ha!, 1948

I have found it better than my dream; for there is nothing else in life comparable … to the thick, heavy, oppressive, sombre delight which an American is sensible of … in the atmosphere of London.

NATHANIEL HAWTHORNE
Our Old Home, 1863

Upon sallying out this morning encountered the old-fashioned pea soup London fog – of a gamboge color. It was lifted, however, from the ground and floated in mid air. When lower, it is worse.

HERMAN MELVILLE
Journal of a Tour to London and the Continent, 24 November 1849

Up to this time I have been crushed under a sense of the mere magnitude of London ... in such a way as to paralyse my mind for any appreciation of details. This is gradually subsiding; but what does it leave behind it? An extraordinary intellectual depression.

HENRY JAMES
in a letter to Alice James, 10 March 1869

I begin to be giddy with the world of London, and to feel my spirits flag. There are so many drawbacks, from hairdressers, bad weather and fatigue, that it requires strong health greatly to enjoy being abroad.

ANNA LETITIA BARBAULD, English poet and bluestocking
in a letter to Dr Aiken, 2 January 1784

The city overwhelmed our expectations. The Kiplingesque grandeur of Waterloo Station, the Eliotic despondency of the brick row in Chelsea ... the Dickensian nightmare of fog and sweating pavement and besmirched cornices.

JOHN UPDIKE on London
'A Madman', *New Yorker*, 22 December 1962

To Stonehenge over the plain and some prodigious great hills even to fright us. Came thither and them find as prodigious as any tales I ever heard of them and worth going this journey to see. God knows what their use was.

SAMUEL PEPYS
Diary, 11 June 1668

The stones I found in possession when I arrived of American tourists, but even these could do little to injure the fine calm of the place ... Stonehenge has much in common with primitive Egypt.

WILFRED SCAWEN BLUNT
Diary, 18 August 1894

The sight of English villages imparts to me a degree of pleasure that I never experienced in beholding those of France & Italy. I form to myself pictures of rural happiness – of comfort – plenty.

WASHINGTON IRVING
Journal of a Tour Through France and Italy, 1804-05

Being agog to see some Devonshire, I would have taken a walk the first day, but the rain wo^d not let me; and the second, but the rain wo^d not let me; and the third, but the rain forbade it – Ditto 4 – ditto 5. So I made up my mind to stop indoors ...

JOHN KEATS
in a letter to John H. Reynolds, 14 March 1818

Devonshire is certainly a fine country, but by no means deserving of the encomiums which are passed upon it; those travellers who praise it so highly must either have come from Cornwall, or have slept through Somersetshire.

ROBERT SOUTHEY
Letters from England, by Don Manuel Alvarez Espriella

The wildest most impressive place I ever saw on the coasts of Britain. A lighthouse rises on a detached rock some considerable space ahead; many detached rocks, of a haggard skeleton character, worn haggard by the wild sea, are scattered about ...; that cluster where the lighthouse is had seemed to me like the ruins of a cathedral.

THOMAS CARLYLE, of Land's End
Reminiscences of My Irish Journey in 1849, 1882

Coming back we met a noisy rabble of tourists, males and females, rushing down the rocks towards the Land's End as if they meant to break their necks, and no great loss either.

REVD FRANCIS KILVERT
Diary, 27 July 1870

This Cornwall is very primeval: great, black, jutting cliffs and rocks, like the original darkness, and a pale sea breaking in, like dawn. It is like the beginning of the world, wonderful: and so free and strong.

D.H. LAWRENCE
in a letter to Lady Cynthia Asquith, 7 February 1916

People say it is spoilt. I still think to catch a mackerel in a Cornish bay the greatest excitement under the moon.

VIRGINIA WOOLF
in a letter to Hugh Walpole, 20 August 1928

Up at 6. Finished packing and rushed down the Truro drive to get some sprays from the bush of white heather.

REVD FRANCIS KILVERT
Diary, 6 August 1870

The months of September and October ... are generally attended with much finer weather; and the scenery is then,

beyond comparison, more diversified, more splendid, and beautiful.
> WILLIAM WORDSWORTH
> *Guide to the Lakes*, 1810

Ullswater ... upon the whole, the happiest combination of beauty and grandeur, which any of the Lakes affords.
> WILLIAM WORDSWORTH
> *Guide to the Lakes*, 1810

They who intend to make the continental tour should begin here; as it will give, in miniature, an idea of what they are to meet with there, in traversing the Alps and Appenines; to which our northern mountains are not inferior in beauty of line or variety of summit.
> RICHARD WEST
> *Guide to the Lakes*

Our Caernarvonshire Hills looked very respectable after seeing both Alps and Appenines; we agreed that Penmanmawr was about the size of Vesuvius, and looked not unlike it one evening from Bangor Ferry.
> HESTER THRALE/PIOZZI
> *Thraliana*, 1787

The road along the side of this mountain [Penmanmawr] is cut out from the rock, just broad enough for two carriages to pass. On the one side is a steep precipice, the bottom of which the sea dashes against ... on the other side is the wild and ragged mountain, threatning to crush the affrighted traveller to atoms.
> JAMES PLUMPTRE
> *Journals*, 1792

There we stood on the Wyddfa [top of Snowdon], in a cold bracing atmosphere, though the day was almost stiflingly hot in the regions from which we had ascended. There we stood enjoying a scene inexpressibly grand, comprehending a considerable part of the main land of Wales, the whole of Anglesey, a faint glimpse of part of Cumberland; the Irish Channel, and what might be either a misty creation or the shadowy outline of the hills of Ireland.

GEORGE BORROW
Wild Wales

Down, down and out of the cloud into sunshine, all the hills below and the valleys were bathed in glorious sunshine – a wonderful and dazzling sight. Above and hanging overhead the vast black precipices towered and loomed through the clouds, and fast as we went down the mist followed faster and presently all the lovely sunny landscape was shrouded in a white winding sheet of rain.

REVD FRANCIS KILVERT descending Cader Idris
Diary, 13 June 1871

Talk not to me of bad roads! What can you know of travelling, who have not gone starving, frozen, sleepless, and supperless, in real danger of death by bog, torrent or exposure. Such is the journey to the Hebrides, and none but the hardy need undertake it.

> JOHN SPENCER-STANHOPE
> in a letter to his mother in 1806

Inch-kenneth is a pretty little island, a mile long, and about half a mile broad, all good land. As we walked up from the shore, Dr Johnson's heart was cheered by the sight of a road marked with cart-wheels, as on the main land; a thing which we had not seen for a long time. It gave us a pleasure similar to that which a traveller feels, when, whilst wandering on what he fears is a desert island, he perceives the print of human feet.

> JAMES BOSWELL
> *Journal of a Tour to the Hebrides*, 17 October 1773

16 September 1848 The ascent commenced, and with it a very thick fog, and when we had nearly reached the top of Loch-na-Gar, the mist drifted in thick clouds so as to hide everything not within one hundred yards of us.

> QUEEN VICTORIA
> *Leaves from the Journal of Our Life in the Highlands*

16 October 1861 I made some hasty sketches; and then Albert wrote on a bit of paper that we had lunched here, put it into the Selters-water bottle, and buried it there, or rather stuck it into the ground.

> QUEEN VICTORIA leaving the royal equivalent of 'We woz here' on the summit of Cairn Turc
> *Leaves from the Journal of Our Life in the Highlands*

I am just returned from a Highland expedition, and was much delighted with the magnificence of nature in her awful simplicity. These mountains, and torrents, and rocks, would almost convince one that it was some being of infinite power that had created them. Plain corn countries look as if men had made them; but I defy all mankind put together to make anything like the pass of Gilliecranky [Killiecrankie].

MRS ALISON COCKBURN
in a letter

We had a view of Fingal's cave, one of the most magnificent sights the eye ever beheld. It appears like the inside of a cathedral of immense size, but superior to any work of art in grandeur and sublimity and equal to any in regularity.

DR THOMAS GARNETT
Tour Through the Highlands and Western Islands, 1798

Picking your steps carefully over huge boulder and slippery stone, you come upon the most savage scene of desolation in Britain. Conceive a large lake filled with dark green water, girt with torn and shattered precipices; the bases of which are strewn with ruin since an earthquake passed that way, and whose summits jag the sky with grisly splinter and peak ... The utter silence weighs like a burden upon you; you feel an intruder in the place ... You cannot feel comfortable at Loch Coruisk.

ALEXANDER SMITH
A Summer in Skye

The steam-boat had left Oban crowded with tourists – some from America, two Germans and a whole legion of 'the Sassenach'. The quiet beauty of the scene subdued the whole into silence – even the Americans who had *bored* us about their magnificent rivers, and steam-boats sailing twenty-five miles an hour. The sea was literally like a sheet of molten gold or silver.

DR ROBERT CARRUTHERS
The Highland Notebook, 1843

There are more rivers, lakes, brooks, strands, quagmires, bogs and marshes in this country [Ireland] than in all Christendom besides; for travelling there in the winter all my daily solace was sink-down comfort; whiles, boggy-plunging deeps kissing my horses belly; whiles, over-mired saddle, body and all; and often or ever set a-swimming, in great danger, both I and my guides of our lives ... I was never before reduced to such a floating labyrinth.

> WILLIAM LITHGOW
> *Rare Adventures and Painfull Peregrinations*, 1614

As there is more rain in this country than in any other, and as, therefore, naturally, the inhabitants should be inured to the weather, and made to despise an inconvenience which they cannot avoid, the travelling conveyances are arranged so that you may get as much practice in being wet as possible.

> W.M. THACKERAY
> *The Irish Sketch Book*

The graceful Georgian streets and squares, a series of steel engravings under a wet sky.

> SHANA ALEXANDER
> 'Dublin Is My Sure Thing', *Life*, 2 September 1966

A few professional beggars come round, when there is a change of horses ..., but are neither so frequent nor so importunate, as we had been led to expect. One old lady had evidently got the last new thing in begging, a letter to her 'poor darlint boy as was gone to Merrikey, and would ye bestow a thrifle, good gintlemen, to pay the bit o'postage, God bless yer bewtifle young faces.' Of course, we would, every mother's son of us. What an affectionate, exemplary parent! When we returned, a few days afterwards, she was again in correspondence with her beloved son ... beyond the broad Atlantic; and, indeed, I have reason to believe from information which I gathered from the driver and our fellow-passengers, that this disconsolate mother writes to her exile child every day, except Sundays.

SAMUEL REYNOLDS HOLE
A Little Tour in Ireland, 1859

'But where, if you please, is the Causeway?'

'That's the Causeway before you,' says the guide.

'Which?'

'That pier which you see jutting out into the bay right ahead.'

'*Mon dieu!* and I travelled a hundred and fifty miles to see *that!*'

W.M. THACKERAY at the Giant's Causeway
The Irish Sketch Book

There are few things in the world more delightful than a drive at sunset, in a bright autumn evening, among the mountains and lakes of Connemara. A friend of ours describes the air of his favourite place by saying it is like breathing champagne.

HARRIET MARTINEAU
Letters from Ireland, 1852

Measured and mapped Connamara may be, but painted or described it never can. Those sublime landscapes of mountain, moor, and mere, are photographed on the memory for ever, but cannot be reproduced on canvass.

SAMUEL REYNOLDS HOLE
A Little Tour in Ireland, 1859

The I.Y goes with speed ... of the HORSES take heed

Dover is commonly termed a den of thieves ... The people are said to live by piracy in time of war, and by smuggling and fleecing strangers in time of peace: but I will do them the justice to say, they make no distinction between foreigners and natives.

> TOBIAS SMOLLETT
> *Travels through France and Italy*

I was imbarked at Dover, about tenne of the clocke in the morning, the fourteenth of may, being Saturday and Whitsun-eve, *Anno* 1608, and arrived in Calais ... about five of the clocke in the afternoone, after I had varnished the exterior parts of the ship with the excrementall ebullitions of my tumultuous stomach, as desiring to satiate the gormandizing paunches of the hungry Haddocks.

> THOMAS CORYAT
> *Coryat's Crudities*, 1611

What a cursed thing to live in an island, this step is more awkward than the whole journey.

> EDWARD GIBBON on crossing the Channel
> in a letter to Lord Sheffield, 17 September 1783

Travellers setting out from Dover agree for their passage in the packet-boat to Calais, which is half a guinea for a gentleman, and five shillings for each servant or attendant ... Before you embark, you carry your baggage to the custom-house, where it is searched, for which you pay sixpence, and sixpence more, called head-money.

SIR THOMAS NUGENT
The Grand Tour, 1749

I began as I meant to go on: sitting in the sun before the Café des Tribunaux in Dieppe in company with a litre of Provençal Rosé, a crisp loaf, a slice of oozing cheese and strawberries.

TOM VERNON
Fat Man on a Bicycle

If there was a noise before of screaming postillions and cracked horns, it was nothing to the Babel-like clatter which greets us now. We are in a great court, which Hajji Baba would call the father of diligences – half a dozen other coaches arrive at the same minute; no light affairs, like your

English vehicles, but ponderous machines, containing fifteen passengers inside, more in the cabriolet, and vast towers of luggage on the roof – others are loading: the yard is filled with passengers coming or departing; – bustling porters, and screaming *commissionaires*. These latter seize you as you descend from your place, – twenty cards are thrust into your hand, and as many voices, jabbering with inconceivable swiftness, shriek into your ear, 'Dis way, sare; are you for ze Otel of Rhin? *Hotel de l'Amiraute!* – Hotel Bristol, sare! – *Monsieur, l'Hotel de Lille? Sacr-rrré nom de Dieu, laissez passer ce petit, Monsieur!* Ow mosh loggish ave you, sare?'

W.M. THACKERAY
The Paris Sketch Book

It has been as much as I could do to forbear putting my head out at the coach window many a Time in the Streets, the principal streets of this glory of the world, to bring up the contents of my stomach, when I have passed by so much liver, lights and other offal, cut out in slices and sold on small tables in almost every street, whether it is for Dogs, Cats or themselves it it equally offensive: the monstrous black sausages, in great Guts or Bladders, hanging by many of their Shop windows; quantities of Sheep's heads boiled and partly dried in heaps on stalls, are all such odious and indelicate sights as would turn any other stomach but that of a Frenchman.

REVD WILLIAM COLE
A Journal of My Journey to Paris, 1765

Walking the streets is extremely dangerous, riding in them very expensive; and when those things which are worthy to be seen (and much there is very worthy) have been seen, the city of Paris becomes a melancholy residence for a stranger who neither plays at cards, dice, or deals in the principal manufacture of the city; i.e. *ready-made love*, a business which is carried on with great success, and with more decency, I think, than even in London.

PHILIP THICKNESSE

A Year's Journey through France and Spain, 1789

I think every wife has a right to insist upon seeing Paris.

REVD SYDNEY SMITH

in a letter to Countess Grey, 11 September 1835

My great terror here is of getting run over. There is a continual rush of carriages, drays and omnibuses through these wide boulevards and avenues. A coachman never holds up for you. On the contrary he will whip up and drive right at you.

LILIAN LELAND

Travelling Alone, A Woman's Journey Round the World, 1890

... that screaming wolf pack of fast traffic that is more terrifying, more concentratedly breathless, more egotistical, more ravening after human prey than any other traffic in Europe.

V.S. PRITCHETT writing in 1963

At Home and Abroad

The shops are splendid, and for show, pleasure, and luxury this place is ... the capital of Europe; and as Europe gets richer and richer, and show, pleasure, and luxury are more and more valued, Paris will be more and more important, and more and more the capital of Europe.

MATTHEW ARNOLD

in a letter to his mother, 12 April 1865

A French Diligence

19 October 1763, from Lyons For my own part, I hate French cookery, and abominate garlick, with which all their ragouts, in this part of the country, are highly seasoned; we therefore formed a different plan of living upon the road. Before we left Paris, we laid in a stock of tea, chocolate, cured neats' tongues, and *saucissons*, or Bologna sausages ... About ten in the morning we stopped to breakfast at some auberge, where we always found bread, butter, and milk. In the mean time, we ordered a *poulard* or two to be roasted, and these wrapped in a napkin, were put into the boot of the coach, together with bread, wine, and water. About two or three in the afternoon, while the horses were changing, we laid a cloth upon our knee, and producing our store, ... discussed our short meal without further ceremony.

6 November 1763, from Montpellier In this country I was almost poisoned with garlic ...
  TOBIAS SMOLLETT
  Travels Through France and Italy

We ... waited in the little inn-parlour for a late train to Tours. We were not impatient, for we had an excellent dinner to occupy us; and even after we had dined we were still content to sit awhile and exchange remarks upon the superior civilization of France. Where else, at a village inn, should we have fared so well? Where else should we have sat down to our refreshment without condescension? There were two or three countries in which it would not have been happy for us to arrive hungry, on a Sunday evening, at so modest an hostelry. At the little inn at Chenonceaux the *cuisine* was not only excellent, but the service was graceful.

> HENRY JAMES
> *A Little Tour in France*

I do not know from how many hotels in various parts of France we have gone forth sorrowing, and asseverating our intention of returning there directly our affairs in Ireland could be wound up so as to permit of our leaving that country for life.

> E. SOMERVILLE & MARTIN ROSS
> *In the Vine Country*, 1893

It is market morning. The market is held in the little square outside, in front of the cathedral. It is crowded with men and women, in blue, in red, in green, in white; with canvassed stalls; and fluttering merchandise. The country people are grouped about, with their clean baskets before them. Here the lace-sellers; there, the butter and egg sellers; there the fruit-sellers ... The whole place looks as if it were the stage of some great theatre, and the curtain had just run up, for a picturesque ballet.

> CHARLES DICKENS
> *Pictures from Italy*, the market at Chalons

... plats of roses, carnations, ranunculas, anemonies, and daffodils, blowing in full glory, with such beauty, vigour, and perfume, as no flower in England ever exhibited.

> TOBIAS SMOLLETT in Nice
> *Travels Through France and Italy*, 15 January 1764

Olives and cypresses, pergolas and vines, terraces on the roofs of houses, soft, iridescent mountains, a warm yellow light – what more could the difficult tourist want?

> HENRY JAMES touring in the Larguedoc
> *A Little Tour in France*

Today for the first time I knew what the *mistral* can be. It blew strongly, a harsh, cold-warm, dry wind that dries you up and discomforts the skin. Also the town is full of dust ... I think it must be the *mistral* which unfavourably affects the temper and manner of employees here. The *mistral* is *agaçant*.

> ARNOLD BENNETT
> *Journals*, 10 March 1924, from Avignon

Garlic there grows wild amongst all the other potherbs – and in such profusion that the foam the Mediterranean churns out on those shores is nothing less than *aioli* so that the strongest swimmers from the unperfumed North in those waves turn pale and sink to the halls of the syrens.

> FORD MADOX FORD
> *Provence*

Provence is a country to which I am always returning, next week, next year, any day now, as soon as I can get on a train.

> ELIZABETH DAVID, writing in 1980

Next morning we mount againe through strange, horrid & firefull Craggs & tracts abounding in Pine trees, & onely inhabited with Beares, Wolves, & Wild Goates, nor could we any where see above a pistol shoote before us, the horizon being terminated with rocks, & mountaines, whose tops cover'd with Snow, seem'd to touch the Skies, & in many places pierced the Clowdes.

> JOHN EVELYN crossing the Alps
> *Diary*, May 1646

The prodigious Prospect of Mountains cover'd with Eternal Snow, Clouds hanging far below our feet, and the cascades tumbling down the Rocks with a confus'd roaring, would have been solemnly entertaining to me if I had suffer'd less from the extreme cold that reigns here ... I was halfe dead with cold before we got to the foot of the Mountain, which was not till 2 hours after twas dark ... The Descent is so steep and slippery 'tis surprizing to see these chairmen go so steadily as they do, yet I was not halfe so much afraid of breaking my Kneck as I was of falling sick.

> LADY MARY WORTLEY MONTAGU crossing the Mont
> Cenis
> in a letter to Alexander Pope in 1718

At the foot of Mount Cenis we were obliged to quit our chaise, which was taken all to pieces and loaded on mules; and we were carried in low arm-chairs on poles, swathed in beaver bonnets, beaver gloves, beaver stockings, muffs, and bear-skins ... We had twelve men and nine mules to carry us, our servants, and baggage, and were above five hours in this agreeable jaunt! The day before, I had a cruel accident ... I had brought with me a little black spaniel of King

Charles's breed; but the prettiest, fattest, dearest creature! I had let it out of the chaise for the air, and it was waddling along close to the head of the horses, on the top of the highest Alps, by the side of a wood of fire. There darted out a young wolf, seized poor dear Tory by the throat, and, before we could possibly prevent it, sprung up the side of the rock and carried him off.

HORACE WALPOLE
in a letter to Richard West, November 1739

We all saw it, and yet the servants had not time to draw their pistols, or do anything to save the dog. If he had not been there, and the creature had thought fit to lay hold of one of the horses; chaise, and we, and all must inevitably have tumbled above fifty fathoms perpendicular down the precipice.

THOMAS GRAY writing about the same incident
in a letter to his mother, 7 November 1739, from
Turin

I remember at Chamouni – in the very eyes of Mont Blanc – hearing another woman – English also – exclaim to her party – 'did you ever see anything more *rural*' – as if it was

Highgate or Hampstead ... Rooks – pines – torrents –
Glaciers – Clouds – and summits of eternal snow far above
them – and '*Rural*'!

> BYRON
> in a letter to Augusta Leigh, 18 September 1816

The Grande Chartreuse has exceeded my expectations; it is
more wonderfully wild than I can describe ... I experienced
some disagreeable sensations, and it was not without a
degree of unwillingness that I left the gay pastures and
enlivening sunshine, to throw myself into this gloomy and
disturbed region.

> WILLIAM BECKFORD
> *Travel Diaries*

I do not think that any spot which he visited during his
youthful travels ... made so great an impression on his
mind.

> DOROTHY WORDSWORTH
> writing thirty years after her brother's visit to La
> Grande Chartreuse

We were each shown into a narrow cell containing a small
bed in pine wood. Despite the noise of the storm which still
raged outside, we were soon overcome by the day's fatigue;
and we were sleeping soundly when an extraordinary noise
startled us awake: the monastery bells, ringing to summon
the monks to prayer, were vying with the claps of thunder
overhead which made the building shake. I have rarely
been awakened in so bizarre a manner: there was something
of the last judgement about it.

> STENDHAL, spending a night at the monastery of La
> Grande Chartreuse
> *Mémoires d'un touriste*

That train worried me, going straight up the mountain like it did.

HANNAH HAUXWELL
Innocent Abroad

… a monstrous caterpillar clinging to the mountainside – Tartarin revolted against the idea of going in this windowless contraption inching up the Rigi's near vertical flanks … And those vertiginous bridges that the train had to cross, with the prospect of a thousand-metre drop if the slightest thing went wrong, inspired in him all sorts of mournful thoughts. Why else was the crowded little cemetery of Vitznau there at the bottom of the slope? … He decided to walk up.

ALPHONSE DAUDET
Tartarin sur les Alpes, 1886

We climbed and climbed, and we kept on climbing; we reached about forty summits, but there was always another one just ahead.

MARK TWAIN
A Tramp Abroad

Mathon carried a lantern till we got on to the snow where it was light enough with only the moon … We went over the glacier for another hour … We had about two hours and a half of awfully difficult rock, very solid fortunately, but perfectly fearful. There were two places which Mathon and Marius literally pulled me up like a parcel.

GERTRUDE BELL

in a letter to H.B., 28 August 1899, from La Grave

We met an everlasting procession of guides, porters, mules, litters and tourists …, and there was no room to spare when you had to pass a tolerably fat mule. I always took the inside, when I heard or saw the mule coming, and flattened myself against the wall. I preferred the inside, of course, but I should have had to take it anyhow, because the mule prefers the outside. A mule's preference – on a precipice – is a thing to be respected.

MARK TWAIN

A Tramp Abroad

The first time I passed through the country I had the impression it was swept down with a broom from one end to the other every morning by housewives who dumped all the dirt on Italy.

> ERNESTO SABATO on Switzerland
> *On Heroes and Tombs*, 1981

The traveller who has gone to Italy to study the tactile values of Giotto, or the corruption of the Papacy, may return remembering nothing but the blue sky and the men and women under it.

> E.M. FORSTER
> *A Room With a View*

… the most glorious and heavenly shew upon the water that ever any mortal eye beheld, such a shew as did even ravish me both with delight and admiration.

> THOMAS CORYAT, of Venice
> *Coryat's Crudities*, 1611

It looks, at a distance, like a great town half floated by a deluge.

> JOSEPH ADDISON
> *Remarks on Several Parts of Italy*, 1701-05

It seems like being both *in town* and *at sea*, at one and the same time.

> J.P. COBBETT
> *Journal of a Tour in Italy*, 1830

Wonderful city, streets full of water, please advise.

> ROBERT BENCHLEY
> a cable sent *c.* 1947

Expected to see a gay clean-looking town, with quays on either side of the canals, but was extremely disappointed; the houses are in the water, and look dirty and uncomfortable on the outside; the innumerable quantity of gondolas, too, that look like swimming coffins, added to the dismal scene, and, I confess, Venice on my arrival struck me with horror rather than pleasure.

    ELIZABETH LADY CRAVEN

    A Journey through the Crimea to Constantinople, 1789

I have been between heaven and earth since our arrival at Venice ... Do you know when I came first I felt as if I could never go away.

    ELIZABETH BARRETT BROWNING

    in a letter to Miss Mitford, 4 June 1851

... stinking ditches dignified with the pompous denomination of Canals; ... a large square decorated with the worst Architecture I ever yet saw.

    EDWARD GIBBON

    in a letter to Dorothea Gibbon, 22 April 1765

When a rainy day comes, the filth is intolerable; everyone is cursing and scolding. In ascending and descending the bridges one soils one's mantle and great coat (*Tabarro*), which is here worn all the year long.

GOETHE
Travels in Italy

Da per tutto, dove vuol!
Anywhere, anywhere. Go where you like!
answer given to Goethe when he asked for a lavatory

Our last stay at Venice in October 1835 did not exceed a week, as the cholera having appeared, though in a slight degree, the fear of being subjected to a quarantine on attempting to go to any other place, made it desirable to depart while we could obtain a clean bill of health. The English fled with such rapidity, that one hundred and fifty passports were signed for them in one day. The Governor, Count Spaur, was panic-struck, and spread the alarm by ordering a quantity of coffins, which were deposited in the municipal palace.

LADY MURRAY
A Journal of a Tour in Italy, 1836

The view, as I have said, is charming; but in the day you must keep the lattice-blinds close shut, or the sun would drive you mad; and when the sun goes down, you must shut up all the windows, or the mosquitoes would tempt you to commit suicide ... As for the flies, you don't mind them. Nor the fleas, whose size is prodigious.

> CHARLES DICKENS suffering in Genoa
> *Pictures from Italy*

Yesterday spent chiefly in following Baedeker up and down Siena, with good results.

> ARNOLD BENNETT
> *Journals*, 23 April 1914

We began, in a perfect fever, to strain our eyes for Rome, and when, after another mile or two, the Eternal City appeared, at length, in the distance, it looked like – I am half afraid to write the word – like LONDON!!!

> CHARLES DICKENS
> *Pictures from Italy*

The common English Traveller, if he can gather a black bunch of grapes with his own fingers, and have his bottle of Falernian brought to him by a girl with black eyes, asks no more of this world, or the next; and declares Naples a Paradise.

JOHN RUSKIN
Praeterita

I went little into company at Naples, and remember solely that the Neapolitan ladies resembled country chambermaids. I was there during Lent when there are no public entertainments. During my stay at Naples I was truly libertine. I ran after girls without restraint. My blood was inflamed by the burning climate, and my passions were violent. I indulged them.

JAMES BOSWELL
in a letter to Rousseau, 3 October 1765

'See Naples and die.' Well, I do not know that one would necessarily die after merely seeing it, but to attempt to live there might turn out a little differently.

MARK TWAIN
The Innocents Abroad

The beggars are teasing and vociferous in the greatest degree, and rarely thank any one for charity bestowed. They ask for *qualche cosa* in a tone half-entreating, half-commanding, and if nothing is given, will pull the gown and seize the hands of a lady as she gets into her carriage. Numbers of diseased objects press forward and display their infirmities in the most disgusting manner.

LADY MURRAY
A Journal of a Tour in Italy, 1836

One foot to Vesuvius. Monstrous mounting. Smoke; saw hardly anything.

JAMES BOSWELL

Here as we approach'd we met many large and gaping clefts & chasms, out of which issu'd such sulphurous blasts & Smoake, that we durst not stand long neere them: having gaind the very brim of the top, I layd my selfe on my belly to looke over & into that most frightfull & terrible Vorago, a stupendious pit (if any there be in the whole Earth) of neere three miles in Circuit, and halfe a mile in depth ... Some there are who maintaine it the very Mouth of hell it selfe, others of Purgatory, certainly it must be acknowledged one of the most horrid spectacles in the World.

JOHN EVELYN on the summit of Vesuvius
Diary, 7 February 1645

Versuvius is, after the glaciers, the most impressive exhibition of the energies of nature I ever saw.

PERCY BYSSHE SHELLEY
in a letter to Thomas Love Peacock, 22 December 1818

It was the most unpleasant ascent I ever made, both from the sharpness of the lava, which cut my feet, and the very long steps I was obliged to take; it occupied about an hour. We had a beautiful view of the bay and islands, and the bright rays of a glorious setting sun shed great splendour over this magnificent scene ... The lava perpetually gave way under our feet, and was so hot that the soles of my boots were nearly burnt off. The gaping mouth of the volcano threw up large stones of fire and red hot cinders in a most picturesque manner.

LADY MURRAY
A Journal of a Tour in Italy, 1836

The Neopolitans call the crater, '*La cucina del diavolo*' (The devil's kitchen). I asked our guide what he supposed was doing underneath. 'No doubt,' said he, 'it is the devils cooking macaroni.'

J.P. COBBETT
Journal of a Tour in Italy, 1830

I shan't go to Naples. It is but the second best sea-view, and I have seen the first and third, viz. Constantinople and Lisbon (by the way, the last is but a river-view; however, they reckon it after Stamboul and Naples, and before Genoa).

BYRON
in a letter to Thomas Moore, 11 April 1817

The passage to Sicily is anything but dangerous ... In all such expeditions, one finds the danger to be far less in reality than at a distance, one is apt to imagine.

GOETHE
Travels in Italy

I was interrupted by one of the Genoese (captains) who came into the cabin for the Spyglass saying that there was a *Sail* in sight. I immediately went up on deck and saw a small vessel coming off towards us from the Island. The Genoese Captain after regarding it through the glass for a moment turned pale and said it was one of those privateers he had been speaking of. A moment after she fired a gun upon which we hoisted the American flag – another gun was fired as a signal for us to bring to which we immediately complied with.

WASHINGTON IRVING

the passage between Genoa and Messina, *Journal of a Tour Through France and Italy*, 30 December 1804

The sight of the Dardanelles, which we entered about 8 a.m., had a strange solemnising effect. Not, however, on those who were still in bed, or on those who stuck in a corner of the smoking room and played bridge.

ARNOLD BENNETT

Journals, 8 May 1927, from Constantinople

We then drove to the Acropolis. Dust. Great heat. The Acropolis and the Parthenon fully sustained their reputation. The spectacle was really overwhelming … What sensations! Extreme exhaustion.

ARNOLD BENNETT

Journals, 2 May 1927, from Athens

You'd think, with all these tourists about, they would build an elevator.

American lady climbing the Parthenon

In Germany I found but little; and suffered, from six weeks of sleeplessness in German beds, &c &c, a great deal.
THOMAS CARLYLE

He said that no man could pronounce German properly without a beard to his jaws: but he did not appear to have got much beyond this preliminary step to learning; and, in spite of his beard, his honest English accent came out, as his jolly English face looked forth from behind that fierce and bristly decoration, perfectly good-humoured and unmistakable. We try our best to look like foreigners, but we can't.
W.M. THACKERAY
The Kickleburys on the Rhine

To be an Englishman is in Germany to be an angel – they almost worship you.
SAMUEL TAYLOR COLERIDGE
in a letter to Thomas Poole, 26 October 1798

George and I climbed in, and sat waiting for Harris. He came a moment later. Myself, I thought he looked rather neat. He wore a white flannel knickerbocker suit, which he had had made specially for bicycling in hot weather; his hat may have been a trifle out of the common, but it did keep the sun off.

The horse gave one look at him, said 'Gott in Himmel!' as plainly as ever horse spoke, and started off down Friedrich Strasse at a brisk walk, leaving Harris and the driver standing on the pavement.
JEROME K. JEROME
Three Men on the Bummel

Russian Travelling Carriage

Bump, jolt, bump, jolt – over huge frozen lumps of snow and into holes, and up and down those dreadful waves and furrows, made by the traffic – such is the stimulating motion you will have to submit to for a few thousand miles. Your head seems to belong to every part of the sledge ... We had, this time, another youthful driver, a rare specimen of 'Young Siberia'. As darkness fell it appeared to us that he was getting a little reckless; but we said nothing, attributing his daring exploits in vodka, or to the bitter cold ... We had a strong presentiment that something was going to happen.

KATE MARSDEN
On Sledge and Horseback to Outcast Siberian Lepers, 1892

And now at last we were in a land without roads – great, dreary Russia. There were only cart tracks across wide stretches of uninteresting steppes, spreading like billows for weary miles and seeming to have no end.

JOHN FOSTER FRASER
Round the World on a Wheel, 1899

It was a very uneventful voyage. The foul winds prophesied never blew, the icebergs kept far away to the northward, the excitement of flight from Russian privateers was exchanged for the sight of one harmless merchantman; even the fogs off Newfoundland turned out complete myths.

> ISABELLA BIRD on her first Atlantic crossing
> *The Englishwoman in America*, 1856

What the agitation of a steam-vessel is, on a bad winter's night in the wild Atlantic, it is impossible for the most vivid imagination to conceive.

> CHARLES DICKENS
> *American Notes*, 1842

As we drew near New York I was at first amused, and then somewhat staggered, by the cautious and grisly tales that went round. You would have thought we were to land upon a cannibal island. You must speak to no one in the streets, as they would not leave 'til you were rooked and beaten. You must enter a hotel lobby with military precautions; for the least you had to apprehend was to awake the next morning without money and baggage, or necessary raiment.

> ROBERT LOUIS STEVENSON
> *The Amateur Emigrant: the Silverado Squatters*, 1923

Probably in no city in the civilised world is life so fearfully insecure. The practice of carrying concealed arms, in the shape of stilettoes for attack, and swordsticks for defence, if illegal, is perfectly common.

> ISABELLA BIRD on New York
> *The Englishwoman in America*, 1856

Heaven save the ladies, how they dress! We have seen more colours in these ten minutes, than we should have seen elsewhere, in as many days.
> CHARLES DICKENS
> *American Notes*, 1842

Lots of sky signs. Roads up. Not very many people, but a sensation of grandness, immensity, lights, heights. Streets full of holes.
> ARNOLD BENNETT
> *Journals*, 13 October 1911

After twenty annual visits, I am still surprised each time I see this giant asparagus bed of alabaster and rose and green skyscrapers.
> CECIL BEATON

It is the only town where one's looks are drawn all the time away from the ground into the sky.
> FREYA STARK
> *Dust in the Lion's Paw*

I remember *not* being surprised or overwhelmed by New York. I found it the way I expected it to be: a kind of immense vertical mess ... set upon a square horizontal order.
> NICOLAS NABOKOV
> *Bagazh*

Skyscraper national park.
> KURT VONNEGUT
> *Slapstick*

The skyscrapers ... stand out in a clustering group of tall irregular crenellations, the strangest crown that ever a city wore.

H.G. WELLS
The Future in America, 1906

You think you could get this view from a mountain somewhere? No way.

FRANK FUSARO
of the Empire State Building observatory staff quoted in *New Yorker*, 14 May 1979

I love short trips to New York; to me it's the finest three-day town on earth.

JAMES CAMERON

It is altogether an extraordinary growing, swarming, glittering, pushing, chattering, good-natured, cosmopolitan place, and perhaps in some ways the best imitation of Paris that can be found (with a great originality of its own).

HENRY JAMES

... a city so sparkling that at any time Mr Fred Astaire might quite reasonably come dancing his urbane way down Fifth Avenue.

JAMES MORRIS
As I Saw the USA, 1956

At night ... the streets become rhythmical perspectives of glowing dotted lines ... The buildings are shimmering verticality, a gossamer veil, a festive scene-prop hanging there against the black sky to dazzle, entertain, amaze.

FRANK LLOYD WRIGHT

In America there are two classes of travel – first class and with children. Traveling with children corresponds roughly to traveling third class in Bulgaria.

ROBERT BENCHLEY
Kiddie-Kar Travel

Into the sticks, the boondocks, the burgs, backwaters, jerkwaters, the wide-spots-in-the-road, the don't-blink-or-you'll-miss-it towns. Into those places where you say, 'My god! What if you lived here!' The Middle of Nowhere.

WILLIAM LEAST HEAT MOON
Blue Highways

Such as it is, Estes Park is mine. It is unsurveyed, 'no man's land', and mine by right of love, appropriation, and appreciation, by the seizure of its peerless sunrises and sunsets, its glorious, afterglow, its blazing noons, its hurricanes, sharp and furious, its wild auroras, its glories of mountain and forest, of canyon, lake, and river, and the stereotyping them all in my memory.

ISABELLA BIRD
A Lady's Life in the Rocky Mountains, 1879

As for myself, I can only say that wonder, terror, and delight completely overwhelmed me. I went (to view the Falls) with a strange mixture of pleasure and pain, and certainly was, for some time, too violently affected in the *physique* to be capable of much pleasure; but when this emotion of the senses subsided, and I had recovered some degree of composure, my enjoyment was very great indeed.

FRANCES TROLLOPE at Niagara
Domestic Manners of the Americas, 1832

I sat down completely undisturbed in view of the mighty fall. I was not distracted by parasitic guides or sandwich-eating visitors; the vile museums, pagodas, and tea-gardens were out of sight: the sublimity of the Falls far exceeded my expectations ... I rose at length, perfectly unconscious that I had been watching the Falls for nearly four hours, and that my clothes were saturated with the damp and mist.

ISABELLA BIRD
The Englishwoman in America, 1856

These then were the famous Falls I had come so far to see ... Well, I confess that as I stood staring, there came over me a sensation of bitter disappointment. And was this all? ... There was a great deal of water, a great deal of foam, a great deal of spray, and a thundering noise ... These were the Falls of Niagara. They looked comparatively small, and the water looked dingy.

GEORGE AUGUSTUS SALA
My Diary in America in the Midst of War, 1865

Greater than cycling round the world is honour due to the man who can go to Niagara and not go stark, staring, raving adjectivally mad! That honour is mine.

JOHN FOSTER FRASER
Round the World on a Wheel, 1899

The Victoria Falls appeared to me, when I saw them in the month of January, to excel in grandeur any spectacle of the same kind in the world. In scenery, the surroundings of the Victoria Falls greatly surpass their American rival.

LORD CURZON
Tales of Travel

She went up the Nile as far as the first crocodile.
> SAMUEL BUTLER
> *Further Extracts from Note-Books*

Nine-tenths of those whom one is likely to meet up the river are English or American. Here are invalids in search of health; artists in search of subjects; sportsmen keen upon crocodiles; statesmen out for a holiday …
> AMELIA EDWARDS
> *A Thousand Miles Up the Nile*

The journey I find briefly set down in my pocket-book as thus: – Cairo Gardens – Mosquitoes – Women dressed in blue – Children dressed in nothing – Old Cairo – Nile, dirty water, ferry-boat – Town – Palm-trees, town – Rice fields – Maize fields – Fellows on Dromedaries …
> W.M. THACKERAY
> *Punch in the East*

To the tranquil, the inside of the Pyramid is sufficiently airy and cool for the need of the hour. But it is a dreadful place in which to be seized with a panic: and no woman should go who cannot trust herself to put down panic by reason.
> HARRIET MARTINEAU
> *Eastern Life, Past and Present*, 1848

When I was at top, thought it not so high – sat down on edge – looked below – gradual nervousness & final giddiness & terror. Entrance of pyramids like shoot for coal or timber. Horrible place for assassination.
> HERMAN MELVILLE
> *Journal of a Visit to Europe and the Levant*, 3 January 1857

It is at Bombay that the smell of All Asia boards the ship miles off shore, and holds the passenger's nose till he is clear of Asia again.

> RUDYARD KIPLING
> *From Tideway to Tideway*

I shall always be glad to have seen it – for the same reason Papa gave for being glad to have seen Lisbon – namely, that it will be unnecessary ever to see it again.

> WINSTON CHURCHILL on Calcutta
> in a letter to his mother, 23 December 1896

Delhi, where I stayed ten days a making Delhineations of the Delhicate architecture as is all impressed on my mind as inDelhibly as the Dehliterious quality of the water of that city.

> EDWARD LEAR
> in a letter to Lord Carlingford, 24 April 1874

The Viceroy took me one afternoon to see the new Delhi. It was very wonderful seeing it with him who had invented it all ... They have blasted away hills and filled up valleys, but the great town itself is as yet little more than foundations. The roads are laid out that lead from it to the four corners of India, and down each vista you see the ruins of some older imperial Delhi.

> GERTRUDE BELL
> in a letter to F.B., 18 February 1916

... a city built for giants ... a city built like a monument.

> V.S. NAIPAUL
> *An Area of Darkness*

We went in a large party to the town [Benares] in carriages; when the streets grew too narrow for carriages, we got on elephants; when the elephants stuck fast, we tried tonjauns; and when the streets contracted still further, we walked; and at last, I suppose, they came to a point, for we came back.

EMILY EDEN
in a letter 22 November 1837, *Up the Country* 1866

Taj Mahal. Notwithstanding my expectations and all the pictures I had seen of it, when I got my first and proper view of it, the view from the terrace of the gateway, I was overcome by its beauty.

W. SOMERSET MAUGHAM
A Writer's Notebook

You cannot keep your enthusiasms down, you cannot keep your emotions within bounds when that soaring bubble of marble breaks upon your view.

MARK TWAIN
More Tramps Abroad

We dashed on to the top of Tiger Hill, which is about 9,000 feet high. As we got to the top, I saw the first sunbeam strike the very highest point of Kinchinjunga – Nunc Dimittis – there can be no such sight in the world. Away to the west, and 120 miles from us, Everest put his white head over the folded lines of mountains.

GERTRUDE BELL
in a letter to H.B., 2 February 1903

The immense cities lie basking on the beaches of the continent like whales that have taken to the land.
> ARNOLD TOYNBEE, of Australia
> *East to West*

I had no idea that it was a kind of glorified French Riviera.
> VISCOUNT NORTHCLIFFE
> *My Journey Round the World*, 1923

I like to think of it as the only Anglo-Saxon country with Mediterranean qualities.
> JOHN DOUGLAS PRINGLE
> *Australian Accent*

It is so inexpressibly lovely that it makes a man ask himself whether it would not be worth his while to move his household goods to the eastern coast of Australia in order that he might look at it as long as he can look at anything.
> ANTHONY TROLLOPE, of Sydney Harbour
> *Australia and New Zealand*

God made the harbour, and that's all right, but Satan made Sydney.
> a citizen of Sydney, quoted by MARK TWAIN
> *More Tramps Abroad*

It's part San Francisco. A bit of England. The flavour of New York.
> airline advertisement for Sydney, 1980

Sydney is exactly like Manchester except that you have the Pacific Ocean at the bottom of Market Street instead of the Irwell.
> NEVILLE CARDUS

Travelling is not just seeing the new; it is also leaving behind. Not just opening doors; also closing them behind you, never to return.

> JAN MYRDAL
> *The Silk Road*

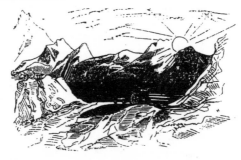

Of journeying the benefits are many: the freshness it bringeth to the heart, the seeing and hearing of marvellous things, the delight of beholding new cities, the meeting of unknown friends.

> SAADI
> *Gulistan*

Now that we all travel abroad so much, there comes a dreadful moment in our lives when our foreign friends, whom we strongly urge to visit us, actually do so.

> VIRGINIA GRAHAM
> *Everything's Too Something*

It is a strange thing to come home. While yet on the journey, you cannot at all realize how strange it will be.

> SELMA LAGERLOF
> *The Miracles of Anti-Christ*